Big Sailor

My First Big ABC

Ages 3-5

Vol. 7 S·T·U

Nachodu!
Your study buddy

My First Big ABC Book Series
Big Sailor Edu

Copyright © 2021 Cambridge Dynasty Press

For permission requests, bulk order information, or any business related inquries, please contact the publisher at the email address below.

Cambridge Dynasty Press
30 N Gould St. STE4000
Sheridan, WY 82801
Email: Bestsailoredu@Gmail.com

Written, Designed, and Printed in the United States of America

978-1-955650-00-7(Paperback)

47678459

Hi! Nice to meet you. My name is Nachodu!

I am your study buddy for this book!

1. Building Skills for Pen Control
2. Recognizing Alphabet Letters
3. Building Confidence
4. Enjoying a Good Book
5. Being Patient with Practice
6. Developing Creative Thinking
7. Being Proud of Achievement
8. Having Fun

This book belongs to

_____
(name)

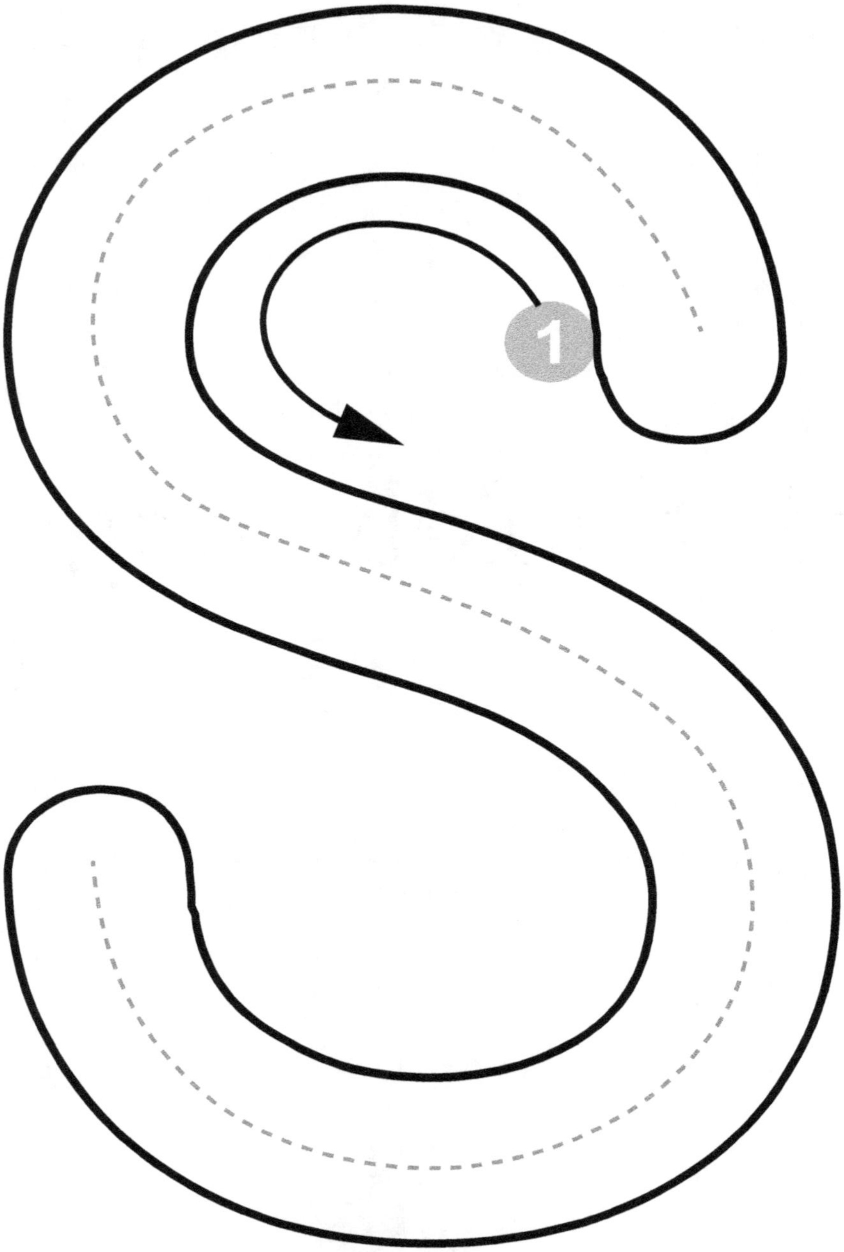

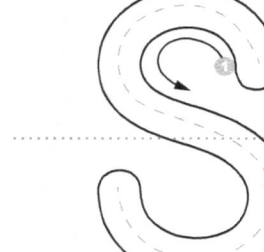 Let's trace following the numbers

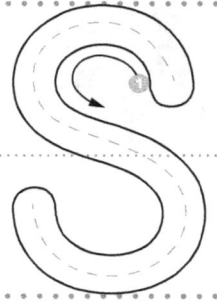 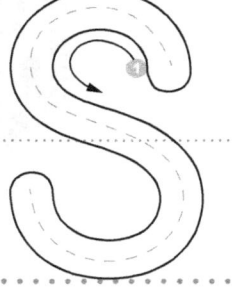 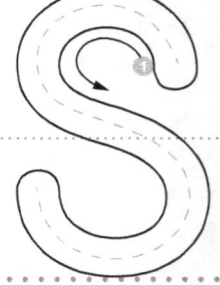

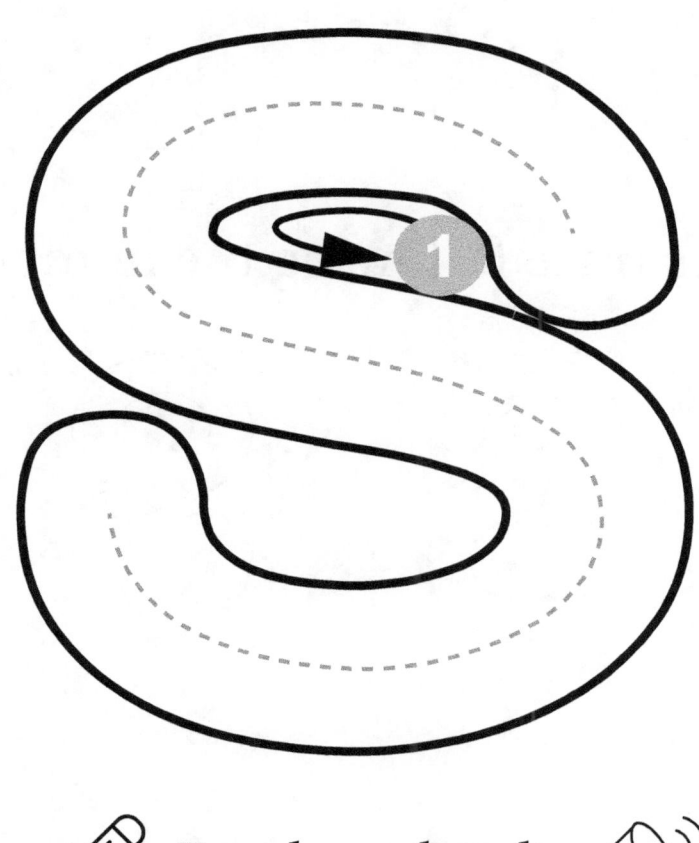

 Read out loud

  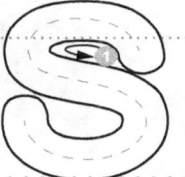 

# Spider

 Let's trace following the numbers

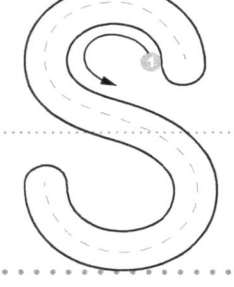 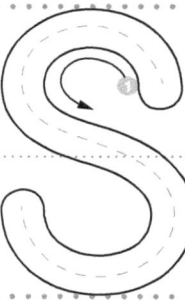 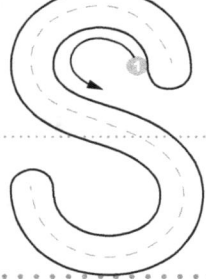 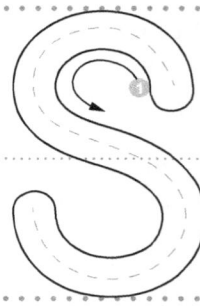

 # Snail

 **sheep**

 Read out loud

 **socks**

Find every S and color them

Trace the dotted line and read out loud

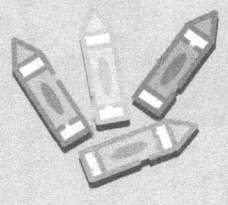 **Find every S and color the sections**

Nachodu

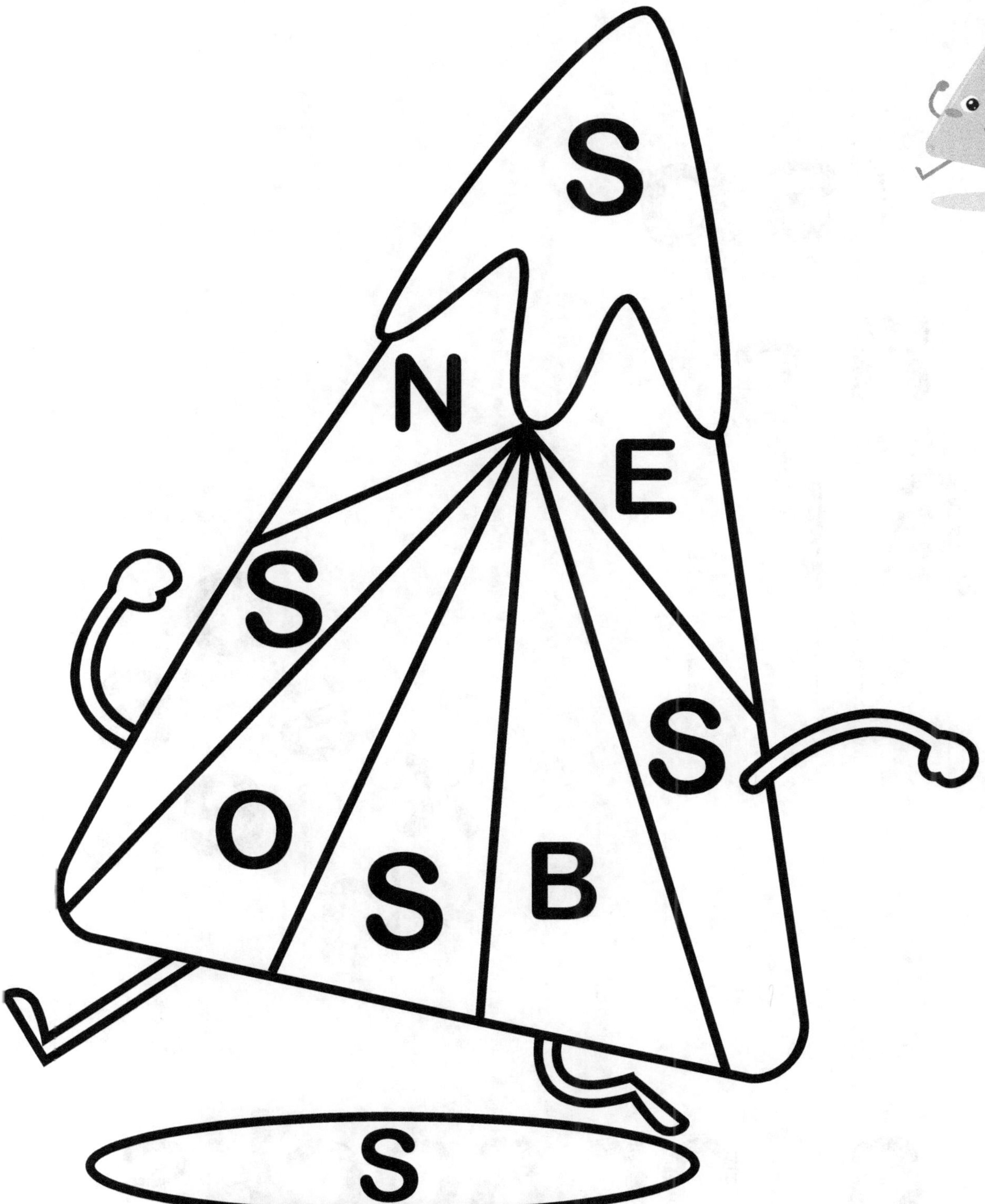

Find every s and circle them

s for socks

Trace the dotted line and read out loud

S for Snail

Draw lines to match

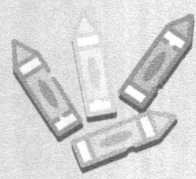 **Find every s and color the sections**

Trace the dotted line and read out loud

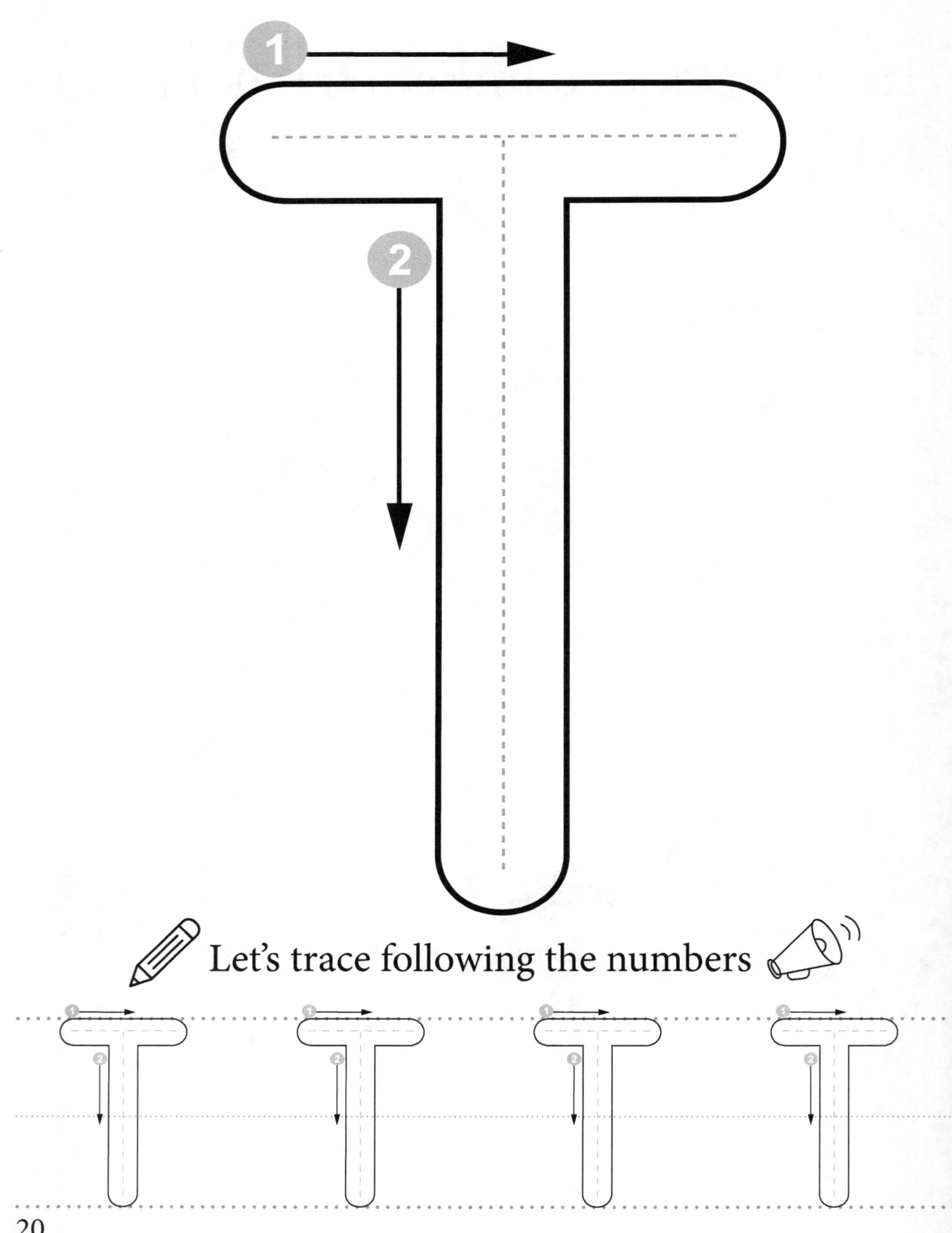

Let's trace following the numbers

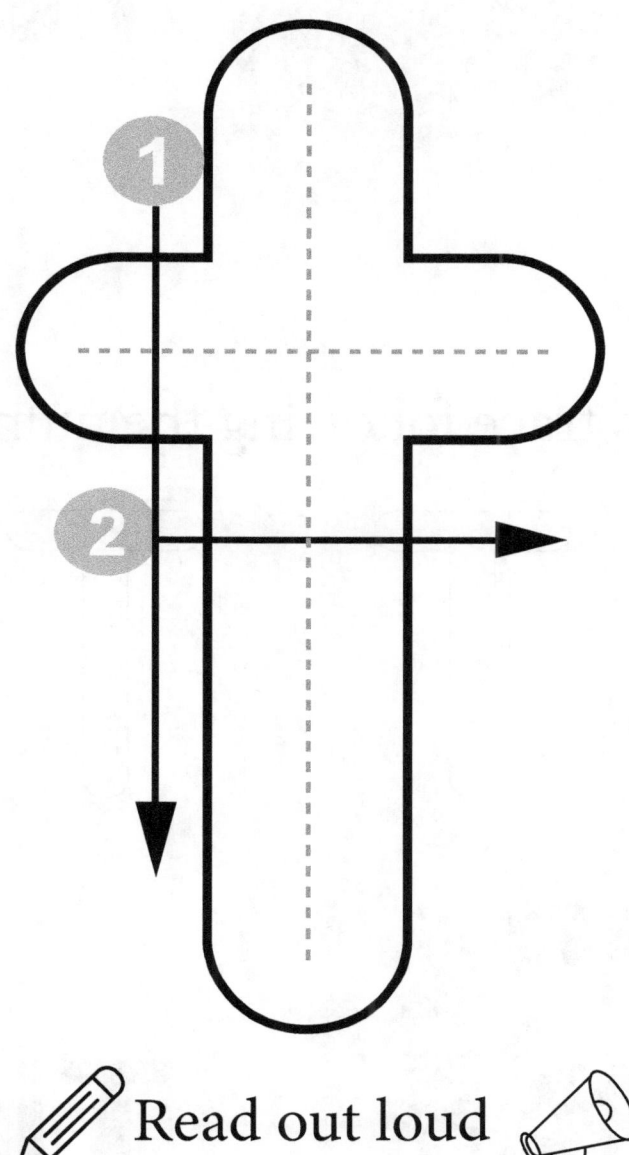

Read out loud

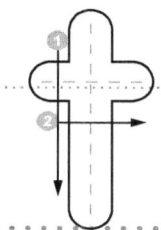 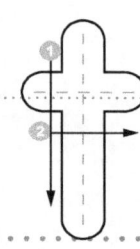 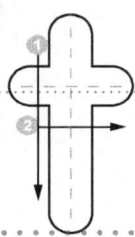 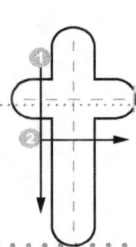

Turtle

✏️ Let's trace following the numbers 📢

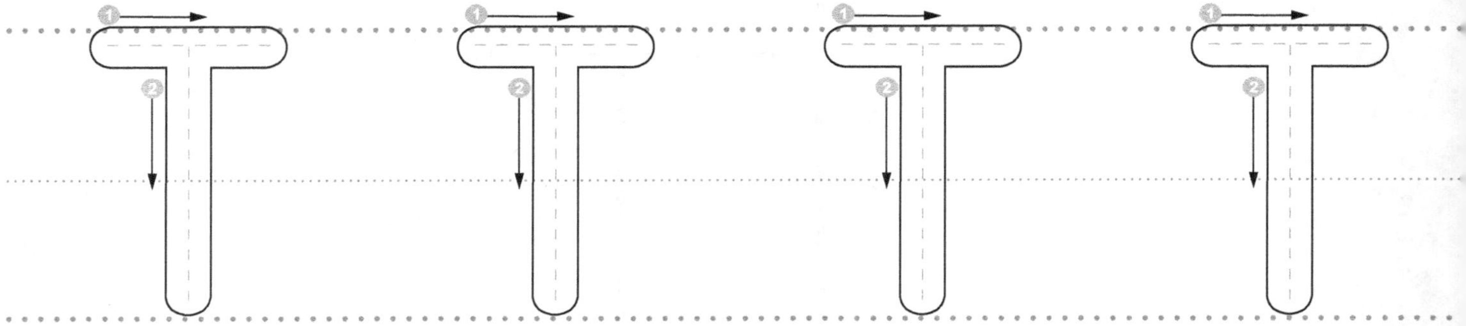

T T T T

Tiger

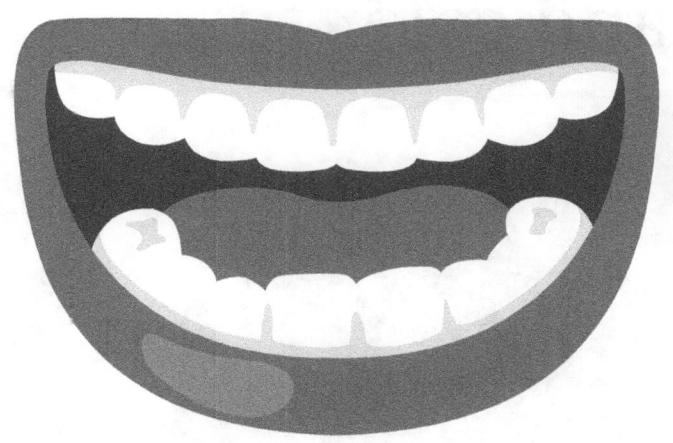 teeth

 Read out loud

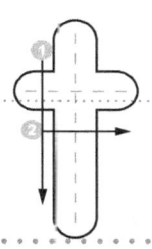 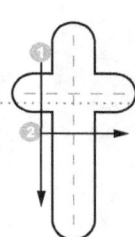 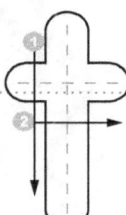 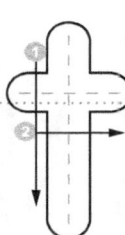

 truck

Find every T and color them

Trace the dotted line and read out loud

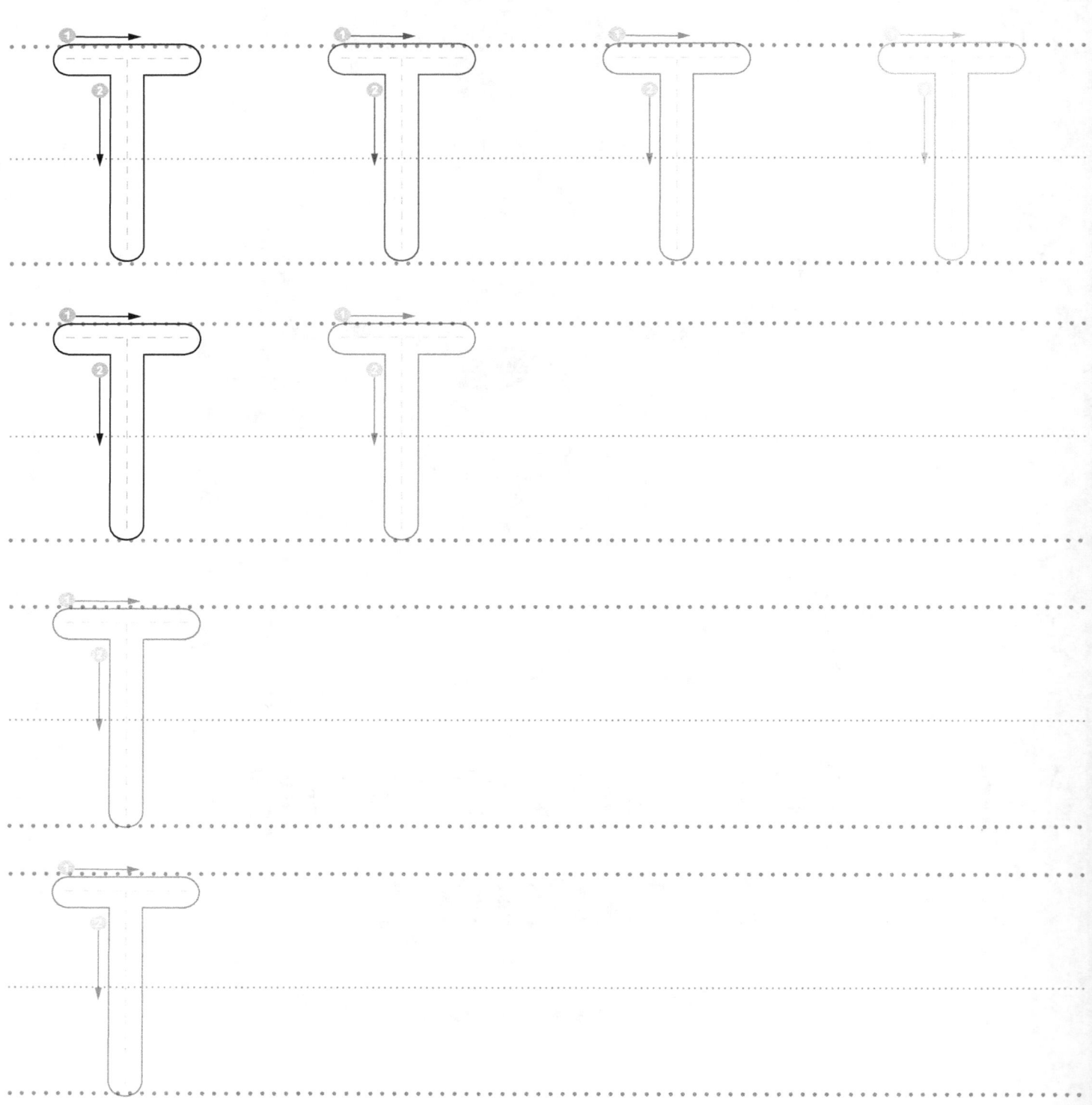

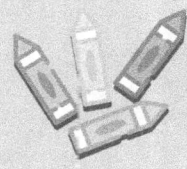 # Find every T and color the sections

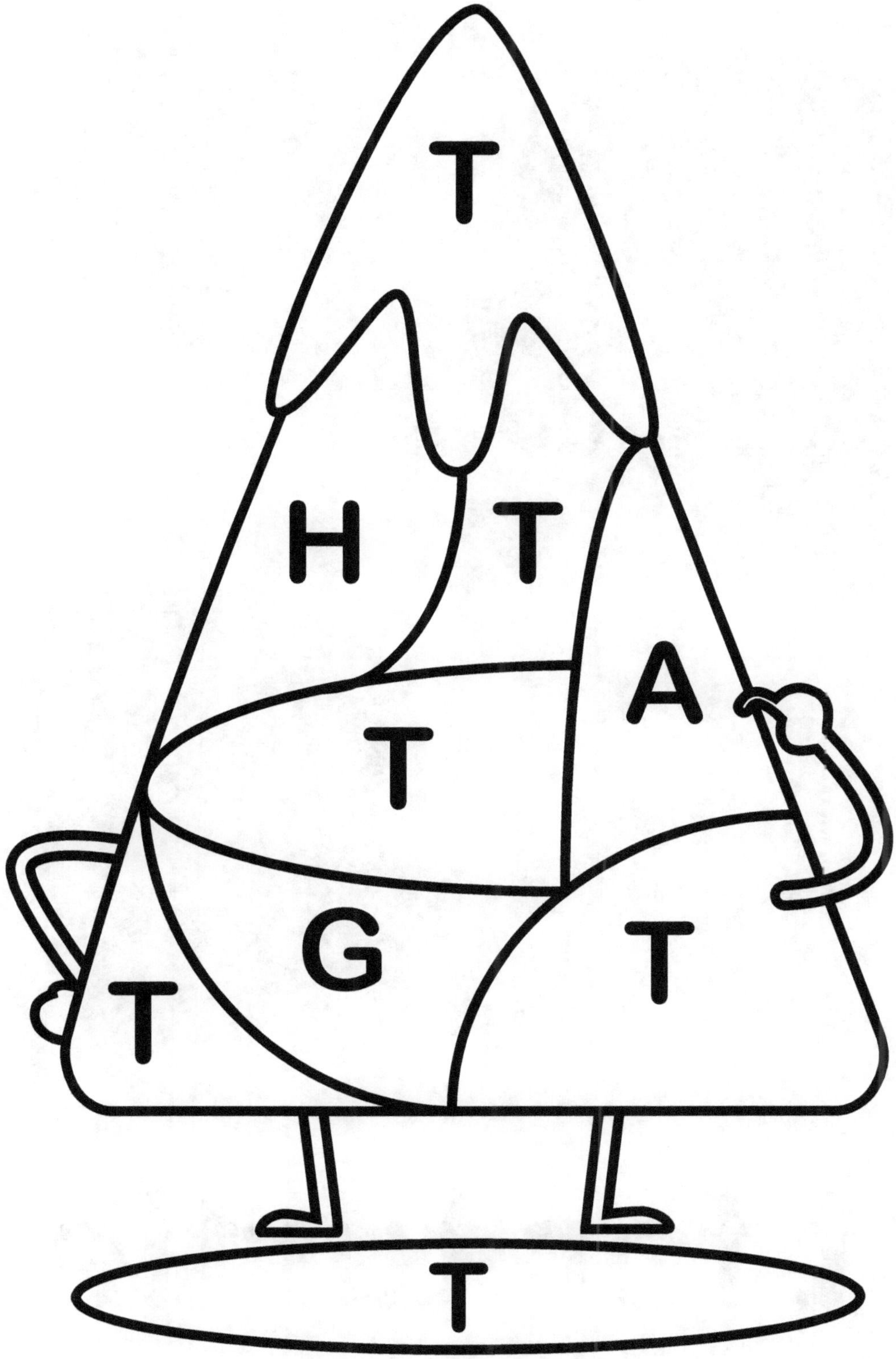

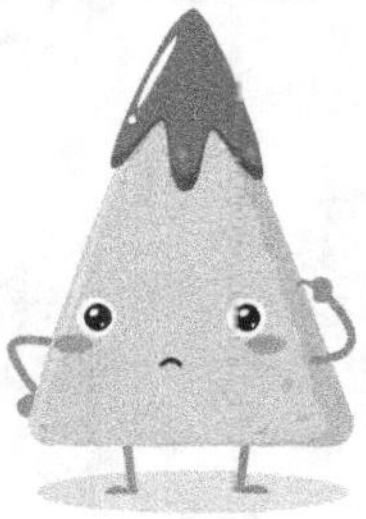

Find every t and circle them

t for turtle

Trace the dotted line and read out loud

Draw lines to match

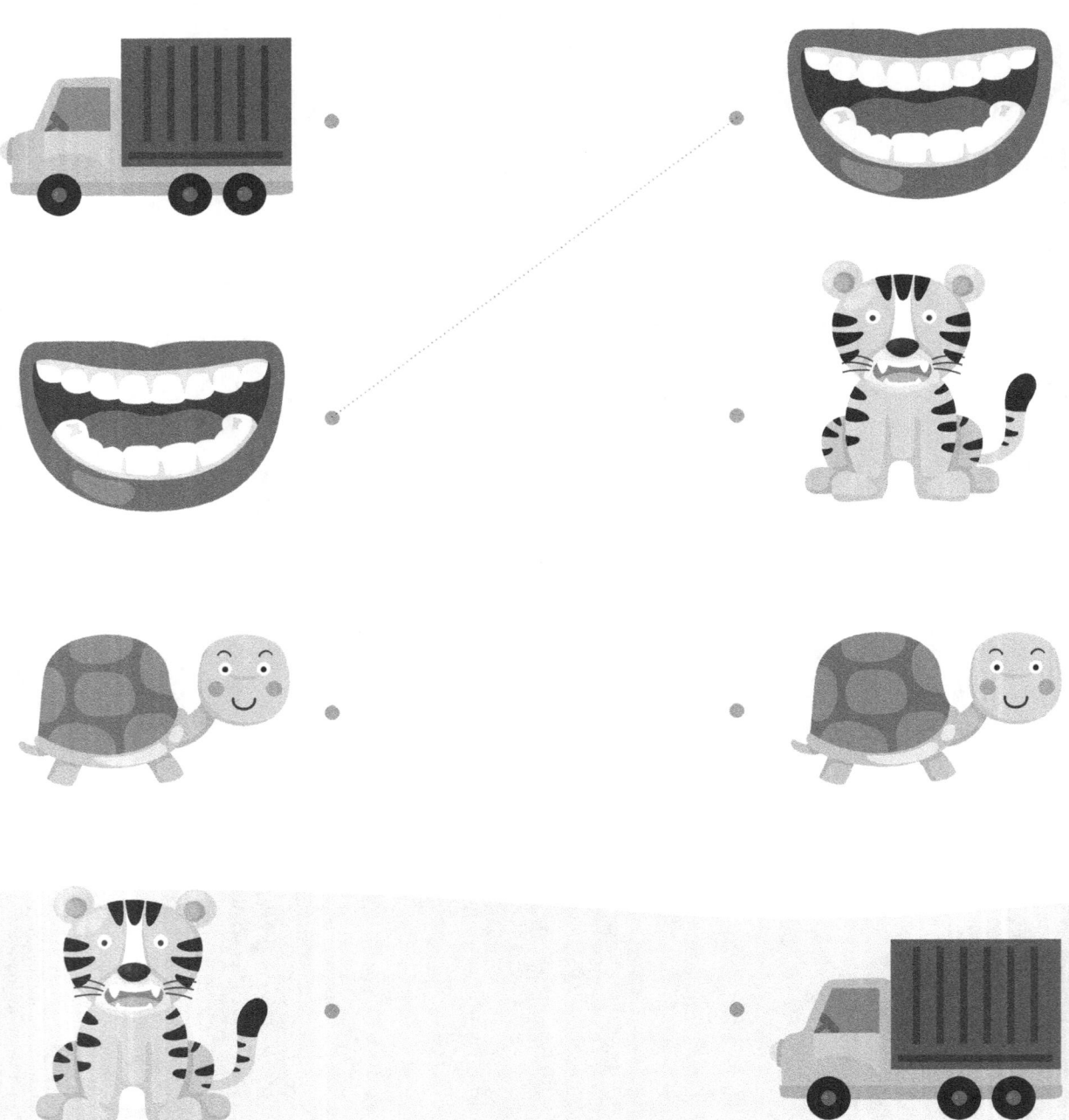

T for Tiger

 **Find every t and color the sections**

t r t o t b t d t

Trace the dotted line and read out loud

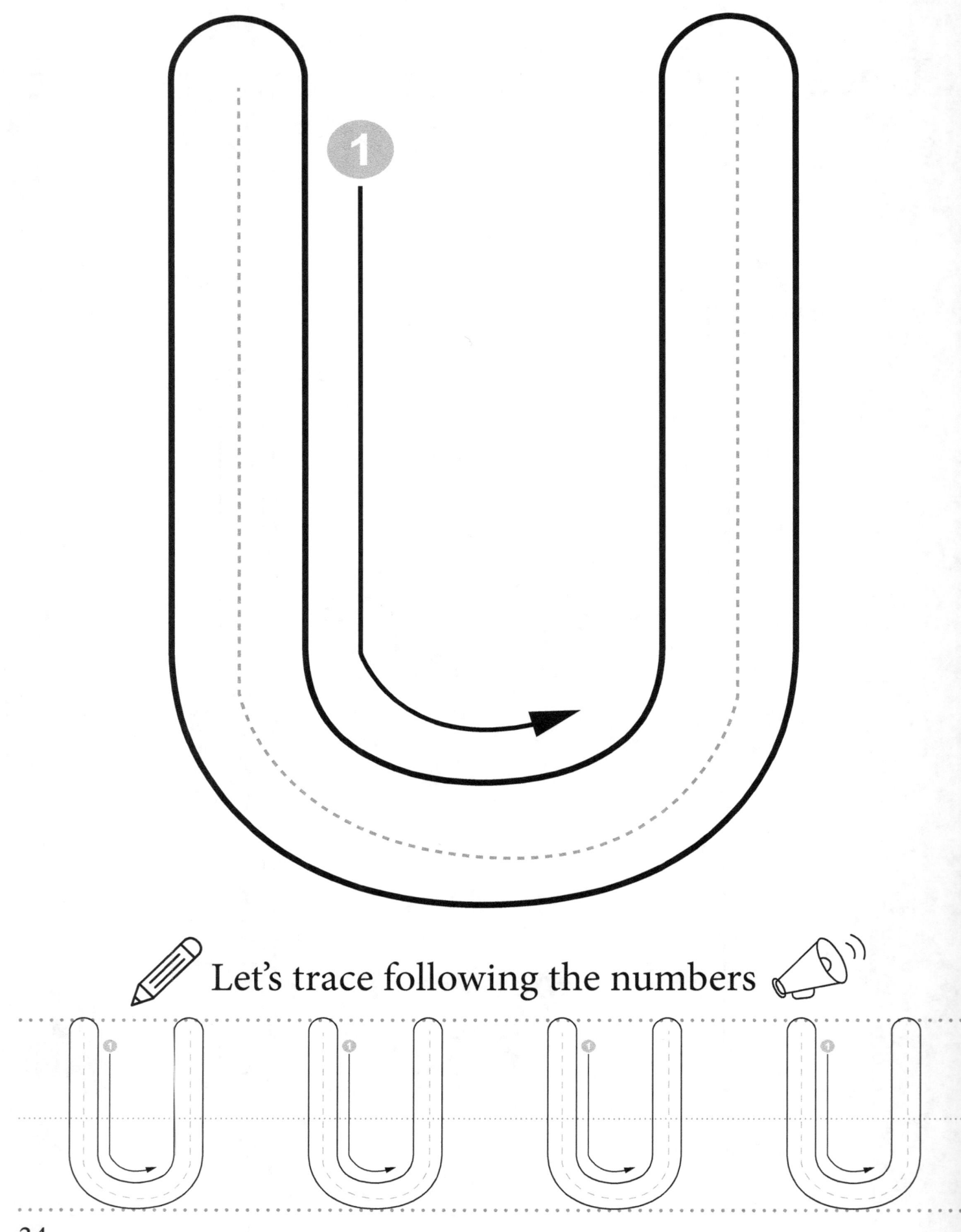

Let's trace following the numbers

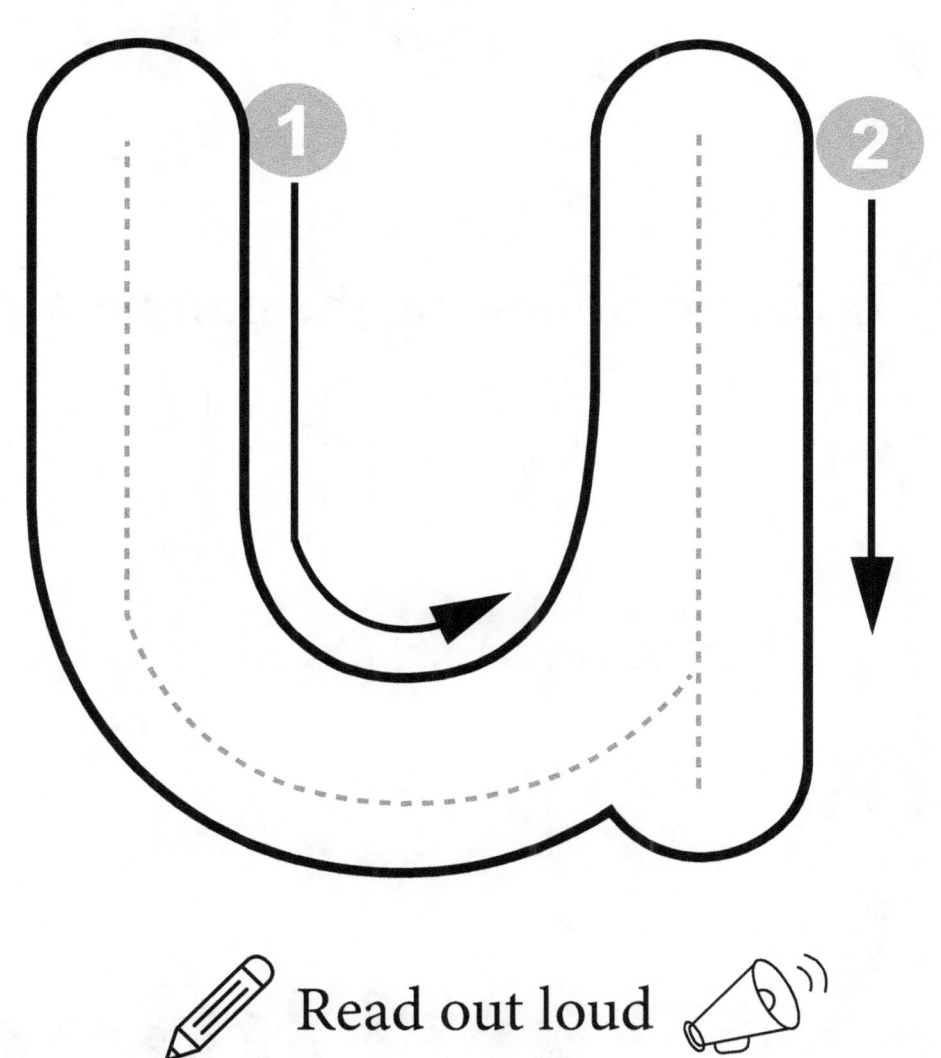

✏️ Read out loud 📢

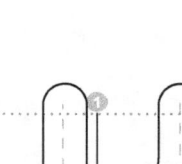 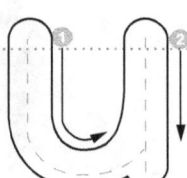 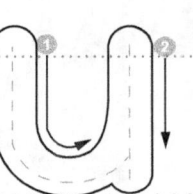

Umbrella

✏️ Let's trace following the numbers 📢

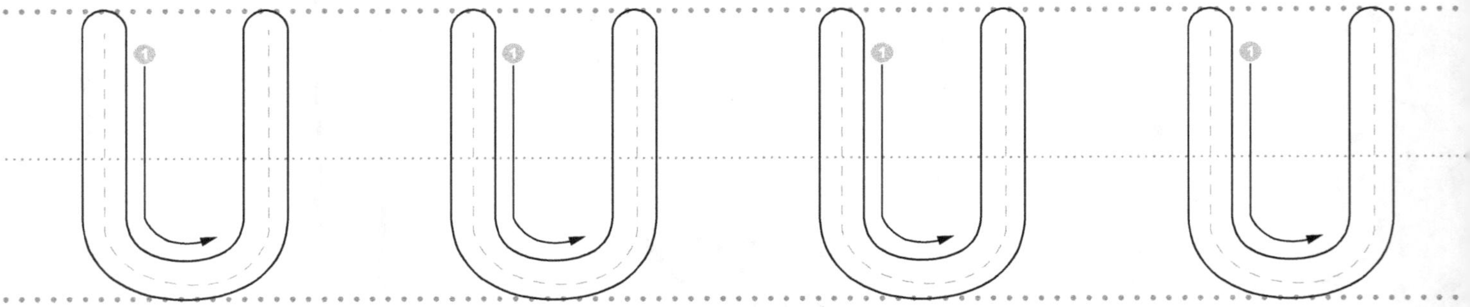

U U U U

Unicorn

 uncle

 Read out loud

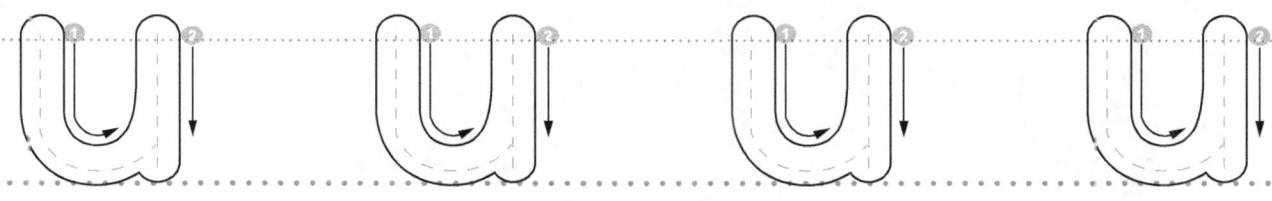

 urchin

Find every U and color them

Trace the dotted line and read out loud

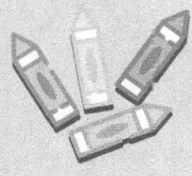 **Find every U and color the sections**

Nachodu

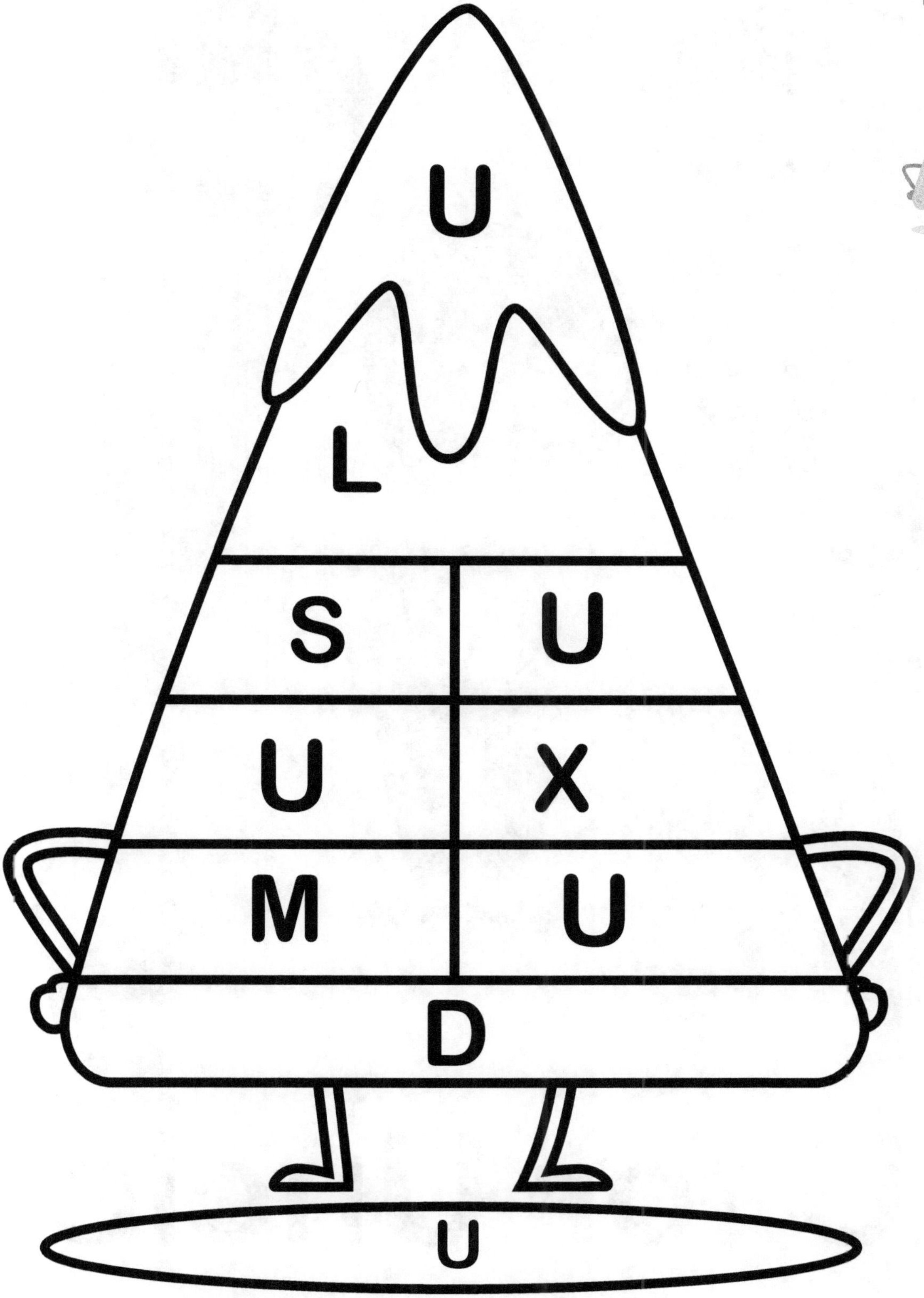

Find every u and circle them

U for Uncle

Trace the dotted line and read out loud

u for unicorn

Draw lines to match

45

 Find every **u** and color the sections

u d u c u
s u o u x

Trace the dotted line and read out loud

Where is Nachodu?

Find and circle!

Let's express your

I am cool

I am hungry

I am playful

I am proud

I am okay

feelings with Nachodu!

I am tired

I am excited

I am loved

I am confident

I am happy

Let's express your

I am sad

I am calm

I am rushing

I am frustrated   I am angry

feelings with Nachodu!

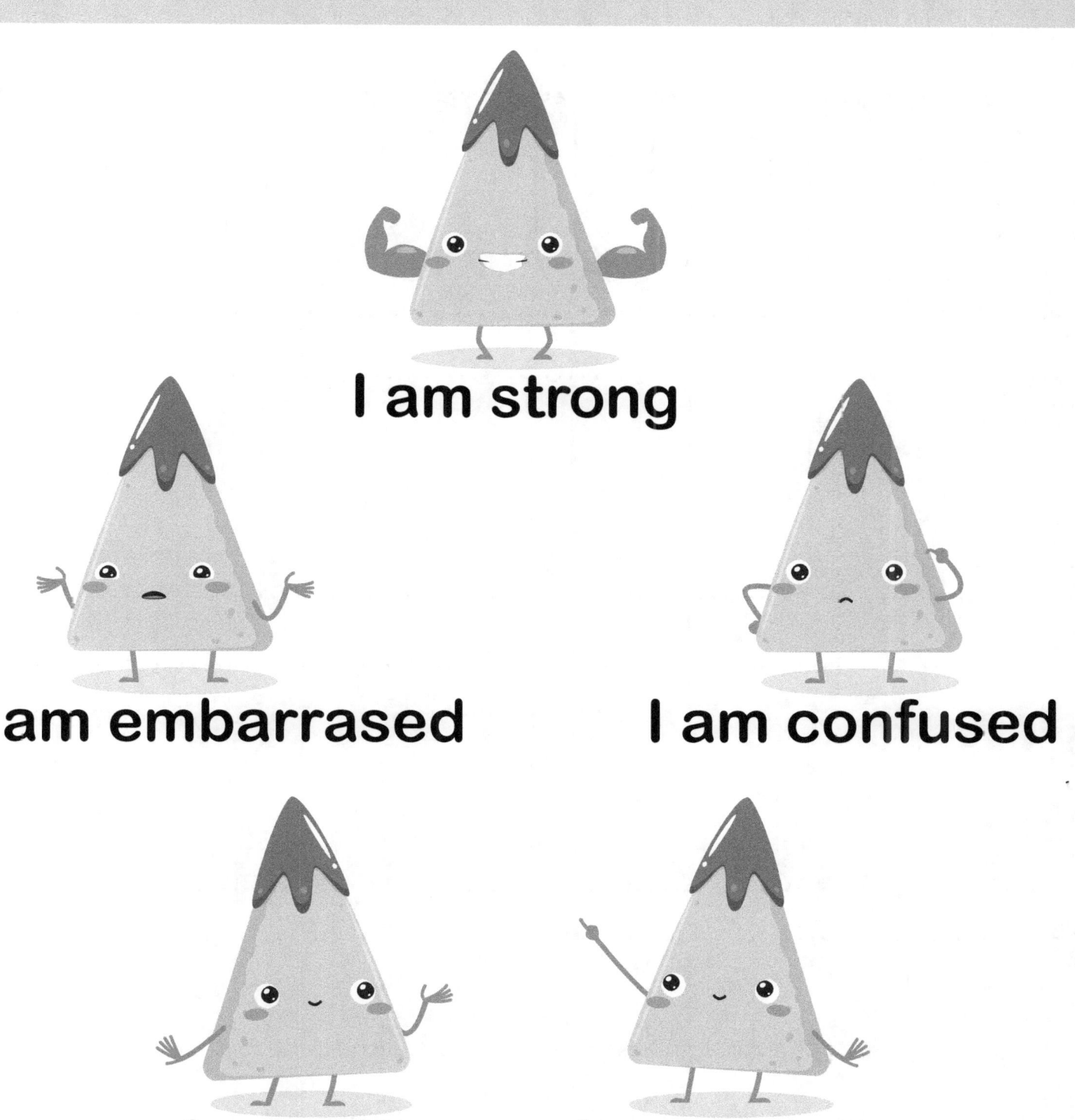

Write STU and read out loud

STU STU

STU

STU

STU

Write stu and read out loud

stustu

stu

stu

stu

Award

You are amazing!

This award is for

_____ _____
(first name)   (last name)

Great job finishing the book!

Date: _____

Visit Our Website

BigSailorEdu.com

and Get Free & Fun

Educational Material

ABC Workbook Series by Big Sailor Edu

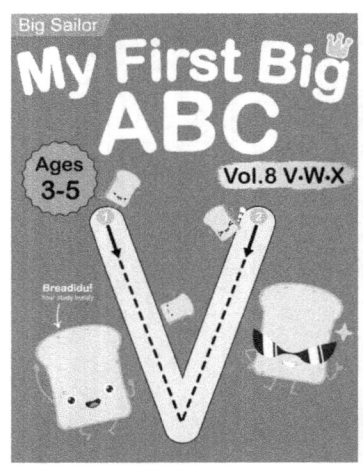